Isaac Rieman Baxley

The Prophet

And Other Poems

Isaac Rieman Baxley

The Prophet
And Other Poems

ISBN/EAN: 9783337047399

Printed in Europe, USA, Canada, Australia, Japan

Cover: Foto ©Thomas Meinert / pixelio.de

More available books at **www.hansebooks.com**

AND

OTHER POEMS

BY

ISAAC R. BAXLEY

AUTHOR OF " THE TEMPLE OF ALANTHUR "

NEW YORK AND LONDON

G. P. PUTNAM'S SONS

The Knickerbocker Press

1888

CONTENTS

THE PROPHET.

THE prophecy must be beyond the ears—
  If otherwise, wherein attain we growth?
There are forerunners : the aftercomers know
A-verity their message : jostling proclaim
With brazen tongues the truth arrived from far.
But how the Prophet and his shaking heads,
Wherewith shall solace his negation wide?
The harmony which comes by death to him
Is useless as a balsam :—if on high
Ring out his sudden words because enforced
By the tumultuous beating of his powers,
When back their echoes drift to him again,
He, broken in the throng, silently yields
Their reputation to the weird, rude winds—
The airs men breathe not—fitted for night and
    waste.
'T is the dark curse of vision cast afar
To fail thro' noisome vapors rising near.
Prophet and man live side by side in time :
Where Reason reaches raises the head of man—
The proud, rude Prophet, driven on the wings
Of blasts impalpable, utters the cries,

That screaming come from some unreasoned
    source—
Himself a hearer in his own discourse.
He with the stricken stands in awe, untaught
The distant course or slow unrolling way—
The time or yet exact fulfilment of
His deprecation or the blind reward.
Two powers upon his soul the Prophet bows
The mightier in submission, daring fronts
Thick whirling darts held in the hands of men—
Staying aloft a sword he only sees.

It is not what we know needs to be told—
When the new cry comes to us we stand a-stop—
Yet he who cries, in ferment of the need,
Desperate outstretches to a halting throng.
Deep in enigma are prophetic lines—
Far from the day, leading the learner up—
'T is unexpected they should be scanned at once.
But in the fever he who calls, athrob
With the great impulse of another Law,
Feels failure in delay and discontent.
Time—time, reward, defeat, and want,
Progress and guessing, death, glory, and crime,
Draw into one the Prophet and the crowd.
All is not bitterness :—some rise enrobed
With hues of happiness and joyful themes—
Some prophesy the Gift and some the Law.
Hoary with song, or bursting youth afresh,
Each is a Prophet and does wisely plot
A long distinction mixed in his destined speech.
Ye, the great movers in the rainbow cloud,
Who sail the dappled currents of delight

Over abysmal plainness of the hours—
Whirled in your gilded visions far away
From hideous nearness of material things—
With palette dyed in day's essential spells—
And ye who purify the changeless limbs
Of beauty from the sweet unblushing stone—
Who sit await with the flush dawn to break
At Eastern gates, and let the glory in
Upon your faces with the waiting light—
What are ye but our Prophets? Never all
Wide-eyed, astound, and wild, but having some
That blink o' the vision which produces
Brighter things.

To dwell upon the future sinks to-day's
Material, worldly things into the past.
But men in journey, weary with the loads
They gather, bend their laden shoulders down.
Lo, the poor Prophet, gazing up and on,
Slippeth the things desirable away—
Unconscious of their loss and his despoil.
Who looks afar stumbles betimes at home—
The nudge and titter greet a careless use—
The banterer and the despoiler wait
On Inspiration and her erring child
With crafty purpose and a sure success.
Where are they—where their gains hideously won?
Blind in the brightness of his consuming rays
The plundered Prophet perishes in pain.
All they divide except his soul—alone
By that the comers after judge and cherish.
Humanity, in light appeasement for
Its blood of martyrs, adventitiously

Writes in the catalogue all pain and woe
For things regrettable, but not of sum
And substance in posterity's account.
Perchance,—perchance the horrid friction of
Despair and agony should be to them
But as the burnisher to virtues fine :
But have a care that we run as the oil—
A polish where some harsher worked before.

Who be our Prophets ?   Are they daintily
Set on the summit of some fashion fine ?
Does the world run long-grooved in a success ?
Up from the opposing side of each conceit
Rises the Prophet, weird, sad-eyed, alone.
In the gay train some prophesy and cry :
" He is a devil—wild and maniac—
We are the guides did bring the people on ! "

O single-handed, stern and doomed to death—
O falling heart and arms upraised in air—
O messenger with message much too great—
'T is but the echo shall achieve the work !

" Give us a Teacher flowing in the robes
Of use and custom—clad in elegance
Of daily profit—and deliver us
Axioms constructed to the things that are ! "

O outcast, needless, powerless, strange, unknown—
Foredoomed to failure and the bitter lip—
Hurled in the invisible hands of Force Divine
Against the seen and dreadful front of men !
How long mortality shall last, how long

Serve visual as the targe of ridicule,
How long the trumpet serve the Sounding Voice,
He who enduring cries dares not enquire.

Struck from the essential Sun of things, is housed
A spark, controlling in the Prophet's breast :
Feeding within—consuming all the frail
Opposing faculties the flame grows fierce.
Like minions to its power, speech, purpose, yield
Intent, time, action, loss, neglect, disdain,
All make in him a destined course and end.

Roll on, O tide, swift with thy numerous prows,
The wind of custom blows on steady sails ;
He who, returning from onward far the stream,
Hails, as an avalanche, the fleeting freight
Must perish, but his voice blows down the gale.
The long-gone, dead, and proven Prophets rise
Figures of envy, and the world does sigh
For chance to fast as they did—and forego.
Tongues of the world are changed, lo, other cries
Come from her Prophets now and go unheard.

There is a time the world shall cry aloud :
There is a time the light shall enter in :
There is a time for comprehension and
Fulfilment of the action unto faith :
The time shall be, as Prophets spread afar,
Men stand upon the pinnacles to catch
Sounds of the unseen Voice, accredited
With judgment for the works and ways of men.
Hear ye—train to the murmurs indistinct
From the far sounds starting in other airs !

THE SOWERS.

WHO knows? The world is wide and God did sow
Blessings and sorrows.   With daily suns the Sowers
Come a-scattering : over all the dust
Is sifted, and turmoil, the struggle and
The stamp of agony tear up the ground.
Fine from the winnowing hands some blossoms fall
As seedlings which the wind bears wide and long.

To me the Sowers came and lightly swept
Adown the hills their stores with open hand :
Singing the Sowers went—and O the day !

To me the Sowers came, and heavy-eyed
Wept as they humbly passed, and halting threw,
With shadowy hands, such seeds—so soon—so soon.

Pass and repass—O Sowers, come again !
I till the earth in shadow, storm, or sun,
Upon the hills my sowing falls, and I
Walk blindly upward—Sowers come again !

6

LOVE IS A GEM.

L OVE is a gem; the world is night around—
  Gloom, shadow, darkness, curtain the changing
    fires.
Doubt hangs askance, and Fear her mantle trails
Averted, wayward, blinding the light with dust.
Obscurely in the clouds Love gathers light;
Thickly and thin the vapors drift and go;
Love glittering dies—revives, and sweetly shines—
Love is a gem benighted in the world.

Day rides apace, cleaving the clouds and air;
Darkness rolls wide his broadening trail beyond;
Day looks ahead—his flaming eyes discern
Love in the darkness, burning weak and low;
Day rides apace, searching the feeble gem;
Love looks and glitters—the Day bends down to
    take
Love onward;—Day pursues, and far in flight
Attains delight—Love gathers fire and flame.

Love in the darkness shines—shines weak and low;
Love in the light gathers the flame and fire:
Love is a gem benighted in the world;
Love is the gem flaming the first in light.

7

THE MANIKIN.

AN ELFIN, DRUMMING UPON A ROSE-LEAF.

TAP—tap—tap,
  The tale is beginning
    With some one gone sinning,
  Rap—rap—rap.

A SEXLESS IMP, IN SALTATIONS AND SINGING.

To sin is good, for sin is change,
  And change can cheat satiety :
Sameness all pleasure doth estrange,
  Sin brings some sweet variety.

Nor man nor maid am I, and pine
  For sin and sorrow as a prize :
Nor man nor maid my arms confine—
  With neither do I sate mine eyes.

No passion lures me in a maid,
  No heat is ravished in desire ;
No virtue have I to degrade,
  No fuel fills my phantom fire.

S

Sexless am I :—sin if ye may,
  Be quick in sin—envious I fly—
Spoiler of pleasures and of play
  Exempted from such souls as I.

ELFIN.

Ho, ho, my Imp, my jealous chum,
  The sight of pleasure maddens thee?
I rattle fast my rosy drum,
  Concordant to such ecstasy.

No flower grows in the garden row
  Too pure to deck a bed of joy :
We Elves with moonlit lanterns go
  A constant fortnight in employ—

Searching the gardens, searching dells
  For downy petals, rare perfumes,
Wherewith to brew the fragrant spells
  We chant for fruit of maiden wombs.

We pray for maids, but older sin
  We laugh and tease with ceaseless care ;
Ha ! ha ! a se'nnight did we spin
  Round the lean ankles of a pair—

Hoary and eld, catching at chance
  Of pleasure with a prospect vain ;
Ho ! ho ! delighted did we dance
  And skip the feathered counterpane !

AN AGED WITCH, WITH FAGGOTS.

Scat ! ye vermin, age defying,
  Age contemning, rabble brood ;

Think ye there 's no pleasure lying
    But below the creamy-hued
Mixing of milk and youngish blood ?
    Nay, little ones, I tell you surely
Of youth no pleasure 's understood,
    Young sinners do repent demurely,
With us no sorrow spoils the good :
We gloat on joy as coming—thoroughly
    Ease our souls of all regret :
Yes we, the hoary, know most truly
    How to enjoy all we get.

[She piles some stones under a caldron, and, placing the
faggots, fires them.]

SEXLESS IMP.

Young or old 't is never changing,
    No morrow's mine of hope nor play,
No Cupid 's in the stars arranging
    With ecstasy the peeping day.
No garland has the sun, and dread
    Uprises as myself I see,
The piercing spirits overhead
    Watch me, forlorn, exultingly.
I cannot love as men do love,
    Nor am exempted—spirit wise ;
Desire walks with me where I move,
    No virtue from me, dangerous, flies.
O steep me thickly in thy smoke
    Of caldron ; let the gloomy blaze
Wrap me obscurely in its cloak—
    Forgetfulness my debt defrays.

WITCH.

Begone, begone, another grows ;
   My art and I our pleasure slake ;
Behold his blooming limbs disclose ;
   Witness his white and marvellous shape :
Fairer than dawn, more fair is night
   With thee companion, and the spell
Distilled to tickle thy delight—
   To fill with love Life's hidden cell.

[A youth of great beauty in form slowly discloses from the
smoke, standing blindfold. The Witch leads him by the hand
into a wood, and they disappear.]

ELFIN.

So—so—merry and sinning,
   Round is the world, and roundly it goes ;
Even the lover the lovely is winning,
   Beauty is blessing, misshapen are woes.

So—so—greatly desiring
   The eyes of the old ones follow the young ;
Money that 's hoarded is spent in acquiring
   Dainties that truly not thither belong.

So—so—deep Melancholy
   Hobbles with Age, but ever anew
Springs on the byways every folly
   Youth can devise, invent and pursue.

[Morning in the wood : a Maiden pursuing a watercourse
therein.]

Flower and zephyr, meadow mild,
  Lightest air, and lightest eye
In fancy hither are beguiled,
  Drifting about deliciously :
For oh, the essence and the air
  Are mixing in such company
No sense may sift them to declare
  A separate identity.
Mayhap my eyes are overkind,
  Or that some beauty lieth hid.
Surely the sweetly freighted wind
  Draws gently down a slumbrous lid.
Is sleep so near, always beside
  The far-off fountains of the sky,
Dripping the potion of his tide
  As their blue courses downward fly ?
Sleep, sleep the flowers ; betimes must Love,
  The watchful darling, drowsily
O'erlook a maid, for here I rove
  Exempt, unbound, in liberty.

[She suddenly comes upon the Witch and her beautiful Companion asleep. The Maiden sees not the dark body of the Witch upon the ground ; her attention is fixed upon the blindfold Youth, whom she awakens by her voice, while the Aged One sleeps on.]

YOUTH.

Sleeping I feel and waking hear
  Nearness of Beauty and her tone ;
These are the seconds ; O let appear
  The eyes of Beauty on my own !

Subservient all sweetness is,
  All lesser—finite—incomplete,
Incomparable is every bliss
  To Beauty's glances darting fleet.

Why, other, should I hold desire
  For ever tenant to my heart?
Love hath some emblem floating higher
  On summits where I bear no part.

O for the pity, deed of grace,
  Unsealing sightless eyes that turn
For ever, ever, out in space,
  Where never light and brightness burn!

MAIDEN, STARTLED.

'T is Love himself, the dear blind god,
  Convicts my plaining, and appears:
I witless walked, nor understood,
  Passing the path his footprint bears.

Am I a maid, and shall I dare
  Unloosen eyes so full of fire?
Does wisdom lay the lightning bare,
  Or courage scourge a tempest higher?
Already leaping in my veins
  The malady, oft sung, doth run;
Unbound he looks—me he disdains—
  Refusing where he but begun.

YOUTH.

Nay linger not—nay, nay,
Nor ponder, nor delay;

Every shadow hath a sun.
I know my darkness waiteth one :
My heart is up, my blood is new,
As flax and fire so darting thro'
My anxious eyes the sun shall wear
Singly the aspect thou dost bear.

MAIDEN.

Nay, I dare not, Love, unbind
Knots I ne'er again could wind :
Nay, I dare not, Love, undo
Those cloudy curtains from the blue :
Nay, I dare not, Love, display
This trembling countenance to day.

YOUTH.

Swear then, by Darkness thou wilt be
Constant to mine obscurity.

MAIDEN.

Constant to thee as fire and flame ;
    Constant as waves to windy seas ;
Constant as daily suns remain
    Heirs to their desert boundaries :
More constant than to drowsy theme
    Are summer bees, and more than dips
The constant swallow in the stream—
    More than the honey to thy lips.

YOUTH.

There is no night then ; never say
A night was night till dawn of day.

Nor ways are dark if constantly
Unvarying shades keep company.
We know not better from the best :
  We speak and tell but what we know :
No sonnet rings that keeps compressed
  More sweetness than blind ways I go.

WITCH, AWAKENING.

O untrusty ! O ye hateful !
  Ever filching from the old :
Deeds of youth are ever fateful ;
  Death rewards the overbold.
Creature to creator yieldeth,
  Enemy is overcome :
Ne'er to purpose Terror pleadeth ;
  Mercy here is little done.
Rage and Pleasure brew the potion
  I distil for guerdon thine.
Do ruby hearts keep all emotion ?
  Nay, a stronger faith is mine.

[The Youth and the Maiden stand immovable in terror,
while the Aged One, suddenly surrounded by a company of
Imps and Wry-Devils, gives direction to the band.]

WITCH.

Seize the loving ! seize the daring !
  Would ye an old grandam whet ?
Must the aged go a-sharing
  Pleasures their old toils beget ?
Must the aged, ever ready,
  Laboring draw their feet aside
That the rapid, sweet, unsteady
  Dance of youth may onward glide ?

Nay, my loving, nay, my daring,
    Age is nurse to many a mood ;
Passion's, long itself outwearing,
    Color lingers in the blood.
Heady youth makes hasty ending ;
    Fast the maid with brambles wind :
Hasten, minions, to my sending ;
    His over anxious eyes unbind !
Imp and devil madly hale him
    To my bony, open arms !
O tender, thorny maid, bewail him,
    Sufferer in my aged charms !
Quick, ye vermin, something stirs me,
    Really passion leaps anew ;
See ! the glorious martyr nears me,
    Bubbles boil my fancy thro' !

VOICES OF INTERPOSING SPIRITS UPON THE WIND.

Something not in mortal vision
    Weighs the forces of the world ;
Good and evil, in division,
    Circling unevenly are whirled :
Builders to the better faster
    Find the rampart and the stone :
He who plotteth dark disaster
    Must with heavier toil atone.
He who formeth perfect creature
    Other guardian gives his child
Thou lusty, lewd, unhallowed feature,
    With the parent blood defiled.
She the milky limbs disclosèd
    Of an aimless, happy Youth,

We, Good Spirits, interposèd
  By the stronger laws of Truth !
We adjust in sweet arrangement
  Works another power began,
Final issues are estrangement
  From the promise of their plan.
Happy chance and happy meeting
  Intangible shall not be made ;
Joy is lasting, sorrow 's fleeting,
  Futures with gladness are arrayed.
Out to weary habitations
  Drive the Witch and ghostly crew ;
Sweetly sound our invitations—
  Them to Youth and Maid renew.
Sing of Beauty to Perfection
  Linked, adapted, silver-chained,
Travelling Fortune's sweet direction,
  By no evil shade detained.
Sing of happy goal and issue—
  Termination unforeseen—
Sing the broken, idle tissue,
  Impotent, of Witch's spleen.

MAIDEN.

Tho' I did not, Love, undo
Those fleecy burdens from the blue ;
Tho' I did not, Love, unbind
The lashes of thine eyelids blind ;
Tho' I dared not, Love, display
My helpless heart to thee and day ;
Yet I journey by thy side—
The morn a Maid—to-night a Bride.

SPIRITS UPON THE WIND.

Passed and passing, still remaineth
  Goodly Powers and Voices clear :
Little waxeth less or waneth
  Light for happy atmosphere :
Seldom broken or disabled
  Hang the wings of Angels good :
Ever rising goes the fabled
  Echo of some beatitude :
Utmost ether constant lighting,
  Flashing rays continuing speed ;
Betimes by farthest spaces fighting
  Champions procure a daily need.

T I M E.

THE old, old Torturer shakes his beard, and
    strains
With sinewy hands his instruments of pain :
No darkness and no sleep of shadowy night
Hang on the orbit of his terrible gaze :
In all the earth but one unlidded eye
Survives in sun and silence, and sustains.
With every morn his scavengers of night
Thrust on his rack the quivering limbs of babes :
With every year the martyrs file anew
In outcry, fury—in phrensy and in fear.
The old, old Torturer shakes his beard and turns
Insatiate every link with sinewy hands :
Down goes the chain, and the old Torturer shakes
His beard in sorrow—some ghosts arise and flee :
Out goes the year, and some depart, no more
Returning in their phrensy and their fear.

BEYOND.

THERE is a land. Its speech I know not, and
   My eyes faintly discern its colors and
Its clouds. What rolls between is sea or space
Unknown. Yet over this daily I cast
My vision, and delight uprises quick
As distantly the forms of fettered hills
To breaking seas disclose, return, and fade.
Aside the hills of earth, its hollows and
Its waves depart—roll o'er the paving clouds :
I rest forgotten—strangely intent afar.

There was a day I stood. Safely my feet
Settled at ease : the far-off summits shone
With radiance akin to grasping—I,
Of old onlooking, felt abashed and near.
A mystery with liberal permit grew
Apparent : flaring the lights of certainty
Discovered swiftly among bursting clouds.
So standing came another. Not turning, we
In silence, with our gaze unremoved
From the clear hills, drew comfort—till desire
Newly claimed hope. Long looking outward they
Traced faintly and did fall : the seas dispelled :
We turned together and remembered them.

There is a land. We saw : our lips refuse
Interpretation, but our eyes return
With inward lids—walking unnoticed paths.

OUTLOOK.

INSTINCT with Immortality the Soul—
  Dashed from the revolving planet suddenly—
Far from this spinning top of Time abroad—
Trailing Imagination's endless waste—
Sets on its journey to immenser spheres.
Absolutely from the whirling Earth afar
With rapider motion we depart at will.
Beacons catch fire, blazing with knowledge new,
Out thro' the fabulous mists as on we float,
Like new created to creations come—
Intent on purposes terribly far—
Invaders out of date in other worlds.
Diffused thro' desperate space on frightful wings,
We follow essence, and Discovery
Runs like a Spirit thro' occasional ways.
This is escape, The World grown old and cold—
Indisputably dead within its sphere—
Draws to its awful grave that staggering life
That on the great globe whirled its circle wild.
Who travel hence fly doom and fly decay :
There is a Promise, the Promise has its Plan—
For this the Soul prepares its widespread eyes :
Outward and outward, far—immensely far—
For Life the Spirit bursts its frightened way—
Shuddering because the World grows old and cold.

JUSTINE.

IT seems to me that I have seen your face
   Earlier than now : have you been here before ?
Are you mixed in the fantasy of the crime—
Wholesome admixture of a little good
With that tremendous sea of insolent
Uprising volume of debauchery—
Or are you come as secondary, now
Printing the shore after the ravaging storm ?
So pick me up as some most curious thing,
Hurled on the margin of tremendous strife,
Come from a ghastly conflict you cannot
Possibly enter—but must watch results.
This is most likely : in this white hospital
You somewhat are at ease—but do you think
You would adventure out to that supply
Of torment, terror, and foul misery
Whence come these relics you do prize so much ?
Each on her shelf—a curiosity—
Labelled with youth and age—virtue or sin :—
These wreckers salvaged—but on yonder sea
Thousands go down who do not strew the shore !
I have bethought me in this idle time—
This season of suspense—half intellect—

Have looked, perhaps, with an immortal eye
On very much, and oftentimes on such
As you—for now I can remember better
You are accustomed in your coming. What
In recompense have you for this pursuit?
Have you searched out the very devil who
Forsook his hell to cast my body here?
I do not believe you 've found him, and will not
So much as hope he ever will be found.
Certainly you could not an instant come
So closely in the circuit of such sin
As gaze on him who ravished God and me—
God only, and the lowest, deal with such.
At any rate, what am I? One somehow
Most unaccountably has held so far
Out from the filthy vortex of her life :
One whose feet passed wonderfully o'er
The home-paths of a gluttonous morass.
At last she 's felled—or fell. Alack—they say—
It is the foreign flowing blood that will
Go wrong. Justine—Justine—savors something
Askance for trepidation and dismay.
Do you agree in this? In that earthquake
Of horror and dismembered agony
I would have split the very world awide
With one great cry—and not so very much
As one still sound issued in protest forth
From the complete unnaturalness of one.
Do I talk well? I passed some little time,
At midnight, learning books would do me good.
Why should I think of how the sun went down—
Why should I reckon up my steps to where
The precipice was and I lost consciousness?

O yes, the world is very full of birds—
Dismembered, torn, I still am beautiful—
Beautiful with the beauty of the world.
Need mine have been a great, a terrible wrong,
To call th' acquaintance of formality
To an hypothesis of innocent shame—
Make judgment falter, and, if possible,
Lay some light burdens on such hearts as yours?
Lift you that burden somewhat—tell me now
What I should do.　Go warlike with the world,
Bearing the gall of deathless enmity—
Cast out of all its beauty and delight—
Held for a menace in unclean disguise—
And this because I was unfortunate?
Should I forgive?　A single, impotent thing—
Imperceptible almost in the world's great eye—
Scarce lisping in the Babel of its tongues—
Set on and crushed by its aggressive feet
For the resistance soft of being so—
The yielding pleasure to voluptuous press—
The blood that oiled its giant, lecherous arms!
You shudder at such talk—so far away
Seems Hell and all its miseries red
From your white life—you are secure?　Look on—
See sitting on your knee some few years hence
Is she who shall, in change of circumstance,
Pay just my debt of cursèd agony
Into th' infernal compound of this world.
It cannot be?　You are too pure?　No blood
Comes from the wine-press as yours is, but sets
Only from age and conservation forth,
With that delightful essence flavored out
So sweet itself demands protection!

Look you—the dark, red-handed, riotous
Villain who 'll speak in Hell's own tongue to her,
Stammers to-day over the name of Christ—
Prattles that word as any other task—
'T will serve for any purpose by-and-by.
I weary with this talk, but you will sit :
You do not further me—you do not say
Wherein shall open out the refuge wide
When I shall gather this debauchèd thing,
My body, back in all its loathsome strength
That will not die.   You falter, cannot still
With all your thinking, coming, find the way.
I tell you that this question 's all too much
For such as sit and watch us in our sleep—
Thinking they bring us easier rest and dreams.
It is the day, the broad and glaring day,
That you should temper to your hurt and sore.
For we can sleep—too happily asleep—
In separation slight of vacancy.
You cannot tell me—cannot profit me ?
Cannot this moment give me sound advice ?
I am the tutor then—learn you of me :
Go walk as I must in the drifting night—
See if there 's really danger in the world :
May be when I am strong I 'll come to sit
About you with such questions as you bring.

SUNSET.

OVER the deep, the shade, and the gloom,
    An island sits on a yellow sea ;
I stand on the hill, and watch the doom
    Of souls as they pass to eternity.
The chasm is wide and the island far ;
    The feet are feeble—the hills are high ;
The rocks that jut on the ocean are
    Barriers the traveller passeth by.
The eye is upward, but never a sound
    Sweeps from the isle on the yellow sea ;
The souls pass on—stillness profound
    Beats to the tread of their long journey.
O golden isle ! O glittering sea !
    So sweet to look on,—so far away,
Why cometh never the minstrelsy
    Of the ringing chords that surely play ?
I see the deep and purple dye,
    The sheen of riches, the golden ways ;
I see the banners depending high—
    No echo one sweet sound betrays.
I seem to go :—the thousands sweep
    In steady movement—footfall long—

Your beauty, yellow isle, you keep,
  But O for the comfort of your song !
Angels fly out to gild and dress
  The wide pure heaven in glorious way,
Never, by chance, their lips express
  The rhythm of one celestial lay.
I stand aside—the thousands go ;
  I look and listen—surely on high
All ministrant orchestral flow
  Their marches and their melody.
Not so, not so ; I stand and hear
  Myself who calls, and one who is,
Like me, a listener for the clear,
  Sweet echo of your symphonies.
We stand, and slowly, by degrees,
  Our brothers pass, and silence leaps
Onward as they their steps decrease—
  Along yon shores the darkness creeps.
We wait no longer ; we renew
  Our journey as the thousands go,
Down—down—the deep, deep chasm thro'
  We plunge to gain the seas which flow
So far in yellow glory round
  Your shores that calmly lie at ease,
With long, long, stretching, sloping ground,
  Flooded in beauty—distance—peace.

UNCHANGED.

THERE was a hill ; down in the heart was fire.
Fierce ran the mountain's blood and broke in
fury
Out : hot hail and dreadful rush of flame
Tore the tall monster's face and shook his form.
Long streams of blinding rage, sorrow, and shame
Ran from the summit sinking to his feet—
The mountain stood in fury—lashed and wild.

Time went and agony ran out at last ;
Smoke and the sullen clouds of rancor blew
Slowly aside—his face and form were changed.
Long lines of sorrow, floods of the bitter past,
Drew channels, seamed with their altering lines
himself.

Suns of the summer came, and wandering winds
Begot a verdure, but the outline was
What terrible storm had left it :—so it is.

When the great blazonry of shaking trump
Shall rattle in the hearts of hills, this one

Will give an echo from its hollow self
As fiery hands, shaping his breast, did form.
Lightning and tempest—lips and a tongue of flame—
Did give him speech—with unforgotten words.
Long in the caverns rang his cries—so long
His changeless ears are closed to other sounds—
High o'er the world he hears not other tones.

ABSENCE.

ONE stands upon the wayward sands,
    His hollow footing sways and shifts,
Seaward his eyes—the world expands
    And settles as the sea-cloud drifts :
Shaken, unstable, sad, profound,
    The seas and shore do swaying spread ;
Drifting and lifting—ahead, aground,
    Falls the white spray—wild—whirling—dead.

Stand thou in Memory's changing shades
    To yearn and anguish ; clear and high
Rings out a voice—and sinks, evades
    An answer—unpitying passes by :
Look out thine eyes—thy hands upraised—
    The drift comes in.   O sway and turn ;
Sick in the whirling, deceived and crazed
    For rest—for sight—yearn thou and yearn.

NEVER.

SOMETIMES the Soul, misused and ill,
  Stands like a vulture o'er the plain,
Marking the files from vale and hill,
  Watching the dying in their train :
With eyes and heart for death alone,
  The cold destroyer unfurls and flings
Expectant, as his victims groan,
  The shadow of his deadly wings.

Ask of the dying who decline
  In anguish underneath their shade,
Whether his sweeping circles fine
  Are lines the stars did use and made :
Ask of the Soul, torn and defiled
  By fury, agony, and fear,
With what sweet promises beguiled
  Wild eyes shall see cessation near.

EROS.

SIN keeps not the World nor Wisdom,
  Love and Beauty bear the burden:
If I sing them as I see them—
If I listen to their voices,
As they journey, and repeating
Tell of what they say together—
If I listen, and repeating
Only answer as I hear it,
If I answer them in chorus—
Some from Wisdom's ranks arising,
From the simple, virtuous either,
Outstarting calls my word a crime !

Love begets all that 's begotten—
Beauty is :—whatsoever lacketh
Is her absence : always, always,
Looks she farther on, and farther
Love is striding, her attendant.
Sin keeps not the World, nor Wisdom ;
One is heavy, one is feeble,
Young is Love and Beauty winning ;

Thus I see them : when I say it,
One from Wisdom's ranks arising,
From the sinful, virtuous either,
Thinking Pleasure drives the day-god—
Believing Wisdom lights the stars—
Upstarting calls my word a crime !

PLATO.

SOME great Star, in the ages gone, grew and
   Redeemed a mighty void with light and life :
Disuse and death, from greater spaces come,
Fell on the world—its light and life were dumb.
Still to my eyes the ardor of its glory
Comes : where 's none the world I wheeling see.

Long dead, O Plato, star, O generous sun !
Eastward, in ages gone, you rose and shed
Beneficence and fulness : in the West
I stand to-day, and over level plains
See shining come your light and strong renown.

DISTANT.

A FAR—afar—
Love trims his boat and lights his star ;
Clouds fly 'twixt me and Love's sweet home,
Thro' these dear Love prepares to come.

Trim brightly, Love, thy burning star,
Dip deeply, Love, thy bending oar,
Uncanny clouds and grewsome shade
Have long thy gilded bark delayed.

Old age ties with its locks of gray
Cables to keep thy boat away ;
Hate and malice, ugly spleen
Dig deep the whirlpools us between.

Cast off and sail, O bravely sail !
Float down the evening's amorous gale ;
Come now, come now, before midnight
Sets in for me, Love, steer aright.

I FILCHED from Fate and her embedded eyes
A brazen key, therewith unlocked the years—
Saw on the pages of my folded scroll
Many long lines with sadness interwrit :
Glory of action—the swift wings of power—
Fame of my deeds—the throbs of victory—
All these had vanished ; in their stead I saw
Solemn regrets crossing the devious ways
With shadows—light from the darkness sifted.

Then I upgathered every scented page
Whereon bright names were signified and set ;
Bound them with golden buckles and updid
Most jealously the least illumined line—
Sped with my volume back to dreadful Fate,
Absorbing to herself the looks of men :
" Behold ! wide scattered thro' my ways of grief
Were blown these pages of unmeasured joy ;
What wrong to thee that I have thinly bound
These precious leaves inside of studded clasps,
And left the others to thy will's control ? "

" For that the Gods have fashioned for thy ken
These images of distant, wayward thought,

And Mercy's self with constant hand has sown
Some broadcast flowers—go, gather as thou wilt ;
Sing then these songs—they shall be echoless."

Folding the precious volume, I outran
A thousand birds on wings of emerald,
Dashed from the flowers low, clinging scents of
    morn,
And moist with heavy dew, sought shaded courts.
Beside a pool, quiet and comforting,
I stretched the volume on my knees and read
These transcripts from the shining tales of truth.

*   *   *   *   *   *

What if yon large, peculiar Planet were
Our home to be ? Regret, sorrow, and keen
Dismay toll in our ears the passing of
Our days—but hope, sweet impulse, and belief
Rebuild their roadways for departing feet,
And populate some aspect with ourselves.
From this bright ball, rolling its seasons thro'
We go : what hinders our elusive souls ?
Ghostlike they pass—untenable depart—
Floating ethereal in ethereal ways—
Gone and received, perchance, in actual—
Now unknown—conduct of palpable guides.
Yon world of wonder—greater than ours—may be
Such as would sweeten all the pain of this.
Conceive, outlined in light—with fire-tipped wings—
Voices grown hardy with incessant song—
Ourselves ;—like birds high in a crystal sky—
Unfettered arching—alighting—flashing—free.

With folded wings—idle in easy paths—
Think of the converse new, drawn aptly from
Discovered maxims of The Great Design.
Beyond, above, high, and absorbing all
Is Love—the prize delayed in this low world.
There, unashamed, shall high-pitched voices call
Her language—with its purified, sweet tongue—
In yonder lustrous World—our home may be.

    *   *   *   *   *   *

There is a power in immaterial things :—
Kingdoms arise upon chimeras ; dawn
Insensibly before the day displayed
And widening-trees torn in a sightless wind—
Are symbols ; but more unembodied still
Sweep current in the World impalpably
The feuds and forces of The Great Design.
Strange, strange and sweet, to sit at eventide,
When floods of light, receding from our shores,
Ebb outward, flowing o'er the horizon's rim ;
To sit with circumambient soft spell
And influence of the absent in the air.
Clearly th' accustomed way—doubt or reward—
Of lips well known stand in their accent by,
And others, of a speech unusual,
Do supplement, as the poised World revolves
In silence, an undertone—concurring low.
Drawn from the combination gentle deeds
Outline their figures to our wayward eyes ;
Glory seems possible, and to renounce
Our footing for the flight of wings—but true.

    *   *   *   *   *   *

There is a Voice.—Who believes unbounded space
Is vacant ?—Sounding without, striking on ears

Fitted to hear, pulsating constant goes
The crying of a Mighty Tongue, and we
Shake sensitive sometimes in its refrain ;
It cries, and we would follow ; who has not
Stood still occasional with lifted eyes,
And ears intent?   Crying in concert rings
The echo of ourselves swift vibrating
Within, trembling on verge of outburst near,
Breaking abroad with rattle, and return.
When The Great Tongue shall speak, we, diligent,
Shall hasten out, fulfilling its commands.
O listen : bend ye long, attentive ears,
Catching and striving for forerunning tones !
Seek thro' the woods and hills of lengthened years,
For echoes gathered in the bygone times,
That ye may know the speaking of The Tongue !
When on the stillness comes its startling call,
Fly to the mandate and return no more—
Watchers and waiters for its Sound as now.

    *   *   *   *   *   *

There always will be some, oblivious, who
Disuse the common current of the world,
And sweep, or stay, as necessary seems
To purpose higher and unusual use ;
Indifferent in the stream such harbored are
Likely miscalled—or, heading onward, as
Thoughtless acquire the customary curse.
Contemn : the many going at a pace
Discern at once : what needs another eye ?
Where none will listen, and where none look out,
Stand ye.   No page is blank ; from every hill
Knowledge is stretched ; unsentinelled are peaks—

Untenanted the quiet compass of
Delightful shores where learning lies afresh.
Interpreters, go singly out : forgive—excuse
Contention and the active raillery
Awaiting on the struggle and the loss.
Nearing to distant things shall such arrive
Acquainted—on swift revolutions of
More rapid worlds their steps are used and true.

    *   *   *   *   *   *

Beauty is bait for Desolation—lo
Darkness treads on with cloven feet, the fields
Gloriously outlaid : Fire and the forms of Death
Settle with roaring over all that 's fair.
Destruction reigns : hills that arose as swell
Breasts of the beautiful, are aspects more
Immediate, only, of a vast despair—
Forsaken lies the land—none walk therein.

Love is a-chill : the long, unsettled plain
Wails with its winds ; Love garbs herself and
    goes—
Sorrow, arising in her tearful eyes,
Runs with its misty rivers o'er the land :
With little knowledge Love looks out, but pours
Constant her tenderness over decay :
Athirst—athirst—the plain revives, and spring
Life and remembrance mingled in fine return.

    *   *   *   *   *   *

We separate are sent—sped flying out :
The World lies at our vantage : we return
With evidence upon our tongues and speak.
Few hear, and none believe : we saw awrong.

Deep on the impress of our earnest souls
Still shine the visions—again we see and speak.

Like to a light, shining afar at sea—
Fitfully anxious in the distance vast—
In the dark world rises an answering gleam,
Love's timorous, low beacon ; and Renown,
Idly afloat, sails to the wakeful star.
Then Glory and her wide, exultant train
Effulgent gather, as the morning breaks,
But we, with watching thro' the lonesome night,
Cannot forget the way Love looks and shines.

     *   *   *   *   *   *

These things I read with others. The sweet book,
Blotting my tears, was ended, and I read
Ever again, while light there was, the tales.
Night coming, Fate outstretched her hand and took
My volume back ; I followed with my voice—
" For me too late—O Love I know thy ways ! "

RUSH ON, RUSH ON WITH HASTY FEET.

RUSH on, rush on with hasty feet
    Ye merry hours ;
Delay not till my love I meet,
And then go slow, and long, and sweet,
    Let happy flowers
Entice your steps, delay, delay,
Then go not from my heart, O day
    Delay.

O happy sun I see her by
    Stand still for me ;
O keep your glow upon the grass,
And let the shade neglect to pass,
    While wondering why
The owl holds fast upon his tree,
Thou golden day so wait for me,
    Delay.

COMPARISON.

A BLAZE within the forest—the wild beast at
its bone—
The anger of the rushing waves twirling a heavy
stone—
A tempest in the sidelong spars—mid-day burning
the plain—
This is the love within my heart—within my life
the pain.

Sweet islands set on gilded seas—the Pleiads in the
sky—
The mountain mists from pines and firs dimming
the daylight's eye—
At eve the bells of straggling herds—Fairies laugh-
ing on a lake—
This is the love would come with her—I dream of
for her sake.

M Y lips are singing—my soul is sad :
    Sing on—sing on—my lips shall cease ;
The far, far future's voices glad
    Are anthems of such souls at peace.
O long, so long, my hours and life—
    I know but Time as mortals know—
They say 't is soon—they say the strife
    Should shorten years—O heart is 't so?
They say my steps are hard because
    The hills I climb look out so far ;
O Lord of Heaven, they say Thy laws
    To us, untaught, stupendous are.
O soul and life—O distance, death—
    To-day is keen—to-morrow never :
I call and call—they say my breath
    Shall pass—the meed remain forever.
I know but time as mortals know ;
    Alas, I know such pain and fear ;
Joy is the promise, the payment woe,
    Yonder the guerdon—the price is here.
The hills I climb look out so far—
    O Lord of Heaven look down and sign ;
If these, my ways, so perilous are,
    Give me the sight and sound of Thine !

DESIRE.

A PAIN—a vacancy—a want—
   A need that rises up to dare—
A heart that wails, and lips that pant—
   A soul that listens to despair;
Eyes that look long and never see—
   Ears that desire and soundless wait—
A hope that turns from things to be—
   A rebel—scaffolded by Fate.

An Angel waits, and far—so far—
   Glory begirts her raiment's hem;
Blindly between flash brands of war—
   If I shall go it is thro' them:
Desire—desire—so great, so strong,
   I must—I will—stand at her side;
I seek no guides in right or wrong—
   My shackles open—torn—defied!

Before—before—I leap and flee;
   Ahead—ahead 's the only fray,
Aside your swords I never see.
   Their danger 's lost—I 'm far away!
Desire—desire—so wild, so new—
   O action—battle—struggle—storm—
If Hope is lost the conflict thro'
   Beside stalks Glory's giant form.

ACHIEVEMENT.

FAR off is death, and far the living after :
    Ourselves do fail—wearied does judgment wait
Unspoken : we likewise cease—silently stand.

Impossible to vanquish run anew
The fiery goads of purpose and desire :
Past vision, apprehension, indistinct,
Ethereal, but obstinate of life,
Resume and vanish aspect—achievement—plan.

Far off is death, and far the living after :
Failure forgetting stirs in our hearts intent :
Mortality and time timid demand
Succor from some : with anxious eyes we search
Another's secret, and—gathering impulse—go.

'T is one : the doer, he who stays, are one :
Desire and impulse rest a-swing the deed :
What holds the action knows the balance sways
Even betwixt the wisher and the way.

THE JOURNEY.

SPEED ! Speed ! The wheels fly fast, and far
   Run various ways—
The guides depart and dash :
   Fly hence—sweet tho' these waters are
Yonder, afar, gold breakers rise and flash :
   Gently these hills decline—beyond in amethyst
      blue
Lie the long slopes of verdure, tangled, fine :
   Thickly these stars of heaven The Giver threw—
Yonder, O yonder, runs new work—a new design.
Speed ! Speed ! arise and half-way meet
   The day undone, bear back the golden flood :
Pour, largely pour, the spoils of his defeat
   Over assemblies where thou dar'st intrude.
Onward and onward speed ! the hurrying airs
   Divide and tremble with the wings and eyes
Of Spirit—each Spirit strives, and wears
   Over his face the fight—upon his face the prize.
Fly—fly—delay, nor dally not, nor furl
   The wings of action, neither decline nor stay,
Rush out—rush out—desire, hope, conquest whirl
   Outward and onward—rise up—away ! away !

REDEEMED.

L ISTEN : in every circuit sails
    Some planet of superior path ;
Glory on glory's lord entails
    Magnificence the ruler hath :—
Far into darkness—high—remote—
    Swings out a central sun, and he
Unscathed thro' mystery will float
    On the wild wings of bravery.

Black are the spaces—dread—unswept—
    But that this king of suns did pass ;
Round idler lights disuse had crept,
    On weaker flames the shadows mass ;
The fearful fade and fail, but he,
    Conscious and daring, flies afar,
Breasting with power uncertainty—
    Thro' nothingness a searching star.

Listen : Strange spirit may redeem
    An errant sun from waywardness ;
The ample chords of Heavenly theme
    Unusual melodies express :

High in the circuit of desire
  Runs intricate reward and ill—
The widening circle's bounds require
  Movements adapted to their will.

We, as we sweep, ascending high,
  Resolving pinnacles descried
Shall be the steps we journey by
  For outlook upon circles wide—
We, as we heighten distantly,
  Dissuade the grosser doom and meed,
Redeemed from simpler monarchy
  Conception's sceptre reigns instead.

RETURN.

SAY not I give—say not my Soul,
  Ambassador of Eastern ways,
Confers—that grandly journeys roll,
  And caravans enriched, ablaze,
Continue from my citadel ;
  And storehouse coffers, to descend
The sweet paths trodden long and well,
  In home of thine having an end.

O upward, upward, from thyself
  Rises a rhyme so delicate.
It charms the trains of loaded wealth,
  And anxious steeds disdain to wait.
Their emissaries fast undo
  The halters of their homeward stay ;
Swiftly descends each happy crew
  Adown Love's nimble-footed way.

Bounding, departing, eager, free,
  Rush gladly out the squires and steeds.
Lightly the charger goes—than he
  More lightly still the one who leads ;
No burden bends, no cruel freight
  Hampers with hardship's penalty.
These served a lord of high estate—
  But seek a sovereign still more free.

THE WOMEN.

WHY one, openly with a shining gem,
    Walks with the other, searching for a loss,
A hopeless loss and old, with thieves a-near,
Trading responsibility and crime,—
Why one should vainly go, I watching, asked.
She with the jewel—for the other's eyes
Continually searching, wavering fell,
Looked with much answer and a low reply :
" My brother took the jewel from her breast."

REVIVAL.

THRO' Chaos and her dark, rebellious crimes
   Goes Memory a-stir—with eyes awake :
Low in her hands wavers a trembling flame
Left by the Ravisher, and flickering since.
Thro' the wild crimson tide of love revived
She journeys to that distant, fabulous day.
Love wore no cloak of passion, and herself
Stood purer than her garments—undisguised.
Warm in her breath the flame revives and springs
As nearer Memory comes to that long time.
Some wandering farther, and with heart aglow
She shall return—guiding a glorious light.
High in her hands over the wondering world
Shall that white flame in marvellous beauty burn,
Till all the red reflections of desire—
The taint of crime—rapine of deadly eyes—
The desperate glut of passion and her wants—
Shall from departing Night habiliments
Of secrecy obtain and with her go.
Fierce in the fury of a passionate dawn
The dark morass shines like a summer sea ;
But in high noon lie all uncovered things ;—
So in the spreading circuit of that light
Shall souls emerge—walking allotted ways—
Its thin, discorporate fusion of delight
Bears up the footing of their noiseless feet.

BELIEF.

BASHFULLY came the Damsel of the Night,
Blushing, because upon the Day too soon
She tripped ; shaking her midnight locks low
down—
Modestly veiling so her starry eyes.
Trailing her shadowy robes she shunned approach,
But passing onward from the twilight shade,
Another, with majestic, even feet,
Walked solitary.   Great, unveiled, discreet,
Sublime in mouth, with curious, destined eyes—
Whose look was increase, but whose color none
Could see, because some far-off things drew out
So much of light—earnest, refined, noting
Not me, she passed.   Longing arose within :
Because she surely went I believed beyond
Was something wonderful.   I turned—but Night
Coyly threw out her robe—its border swept
My forehead daintily—and soon I slept.

SLAVERY.

AND for her terrible eyes were set so wise—
Such spread of passion on her steadfast face—
So much immovable her needless lips
In telling aught unto her bondsman—me—
And for in that I had been heretofore
Myself omnipotent, I served the more.
It is a desperate thing to be enslaved
In public ignominy ; walk and wait
Mesmeric to contemptuous idleness
Of ordering ; but my impotent feet set out—
Throughout the scandal and the hissing tongues—
The gibes of knots, and single sidelong eyes—
On any purport invented in her heart.
If I had been transferred to some new sphere—
Been taken in the helplessness of death—
And so submitted in an unknown realm
Under the abject dominion of a thing
Beautiful, novel, passionate, and powerful—
Without the possibility of revolt—
One lone one of my kind in all that sphere—
I could have served her no more totally.
It would have been relief to be a slave
'Lone in some other world—the only one—
'T would be th' excuse of curiosity,
And I be pardoned an unusual thing.
But here, with other men, aged and young,

With other women in wide-eyed surprise,
With all th' accustomed, terrible by-words,
Was like the horror of acquainted ghosts.
If I did sleep it was because her eyes
Drew scornful off and I was chilled to sleep :
My dreams were torture, for I feared to be
Absent her beckoning, and waked as one
Who hurries on unstable footing forth
Over the toilsome journey brought him down.
To die was uninviting, for my Soul
It was that served her—that would, itself, return :—
My body was a shield between my Soul
And her.   If it were cast away my Soul
Would writhe in open, endless agony.
Nor did I think of any sort release—
She was so beautiful : sometimes myself
Rung with delighted laughter, for I was
So much her own I could not be put off.
I served and serve : I do not justly know
Whether she is the same to-day, because
I have not for these many years dared look
Into her face.   What she desires I do,
Nor ever need encounter those fierce eyes.
It may be I am changed, but if it be
There are no means for me to know it, for
I will not look on other face than hers—
And that is all impossible for years.

PREDESTINATION.

ON prosperous instant came a Messenger—
   Who was an Influence, or Thought, or Sight—
To draw the veil of hampering consequence
And serious uncertainties of form
Aside, bidding existence far removed
Display its possibilities and shape,
And force the circumstance wherein we sat
Vacate its action of reality.
Into the case of being hastily
Arose myself in part improbable,
Joined with like issues in another.   Which,
As I was in fervid expectancy—
Was molten in the outlook for delight—
Worked in the crucible of curious years
And therefore fitted for the stamp of Fate—
Wears everlasting current in my mind.

THE KISS.

SHALL I at parting touch thy lips—shall we
Consider Time as vacant and decoy
From the slow, inconsiderate afterwards
Its heedless ecstasy and ripe delay ?
No words are contrary, but shadows move
With unkind semblances between ourselves,
Which in the light will fail : and shall we now
Burn up the gloom with fury counterpart ?
Lo ! yonder is the light but never flame—
And we are fearful ; and so further on
And on Love travels with her lips untouched.

QUESTION.

D OWN the long avenues—thro' sightless ways—
    Lost in a distance indescribable—
Circuits where swing the rampant stars and spheres—
Beyond belief—gazing impossibly
On things remote—wide, weird, and wonderful,
I look—whirled on a darkened ball.
Why stand my feet on ruin overgrown
With evil slime, and why poured out abroad
Rolls from the underworld her massed despair?
Thither in scattered glory, stretched so far,
Eternity shall travel without stop;
Speed the white worlds in radiant roundelay
Of motion musical and purpose mild.
Grinding repulsive o'er her granite way
Goes Earth, laborious round her far-set Sun;
Her terrible revolutions of dismay
Earning with agony, enclosed in clouds.
The populace of that tremendous plain
I scan. Each white, desirable sphere
Of those that are widespread in hollow space—
Patching the gloomiest horizon out
Where worlds and millions people airs unknown—
Is as a star—bright to the blotted Earth.
Lonely, adverse, sullen, unpolished, rude,
Standing a fragment, jarring the wheels of Fate,

Housed in a home of doubt and far delay,
O'er those expecting globes my vision goes.
The ready worlds remain and I go whither ?
Some on those massy spheres shall rise to meet
My entering Soul, speaking in kindred tongue,
Saying securely—Thou hast come with us !

ATTAINMENT.

BUT all the world is wearied with unrest :
    Her tortured men arise and walk abroad
The troubled Earth—with messages, but silent.
Silence and speech incomprehensibly
Are devastation and terrible hurt
Of failure as they struggle and they go.
In the sad interchange occasional
Arrests befall unhappy wanderers ;
And some in one way cease, some in another.
I was a vexed and sad, disrupted Soul,
Incessantly and ever in detail
Of horrid search and stubborn agony,
Traversing avenues and tangled ways.
Weary with the wide circuits of despair
I sifted all determinations out,
But one refused—Love and its soul of Life.
Before this Phantom I sat down to die—
For it remained in deadly enmity,
And I forgot all others in its issue.
There are unnumbered phalanxes and forms
Of agony, and every kind dismay,
And danger, and a wantonness of hurt,
And blasphemy most singular of woe,
And an exhausted patience all unknown,

Serve as temptations and as ministers
To such as I—before this Phantom fixed.
But every other energy and shape
Had vanished as I wished, and this alone
Remained because of answer on her lips—
Which I, seeing within, sat down before.
Men thought me dead, but still I staid as stone—
Which has, itself, but one attraction.
No active agony in time beset
My vacancy, because so evident
The desperate forgetfulness of things
Was on my heart ; and in my eyes alone
The only image was impossible Life—
For soul and body are the same in Love.
When I had passed sensation and could know
Love's thoughts as words and words as nothingness,
And neither for the least essential thing,
She spake the first time in forgotten years :
" Thou art passed out except this great desire ;
Therefore naught hinders thee to join with me—
Seize thou desire and find itself alive."

APPARITION.

SO in my exultation I forgot
   Unnecessary forms, and looking back
Felt that most fearful Apparition ever
Was instinct with habiliments and sight.
The Soul of Life and Its Appearance was
To me a possible thing—not creed nor belief.
Myself and all that moved I saw anew :
Evil was passive, and the grandeur moved
Of certain acquisition to the good
Like a strong light, breaking between defiles.
My fellow-man was dreadful nevermore
In form nor action, but appeared as one
Standing unnecessarily in sight—
Because of custom—which would vanish soon.
Myself was an identity unhoused
From obscuration of an idle use
Grown formal, and in governance of laws
More absolute because uncharactered.
Which was a dreadful absolution—all :
Having the trade of knowledge for belief :—
Binding myself in the unspeakable course
Of universal action and advance.
But in the liberation awe was saved
From a destruction too omnipotent
Because I did become part of another—
Which broke the dreadful disembodiment :
But Life hereafter was an endless thing.

APPLICATION.

A ND by a Light so awful interchange
    All ordinary things and usual deeds :
The long, unstinted end of every thing
Comes into view, passing the daily turns.
In haste and hurry roll on thronging years,
And we, with speedier consequence, alight
Over the utmost century and see
Action and form merge into a desire—
Which clothes itself as such desires appear.

TRANSFER.

LIKEWISE—guests in an adequate circum-
stance—
Embodied in sufficient harmony
Of knowledge and of custom—operate
In their own usual spheres the dead of Earth—
Safely related to surrounding needs.
But as they go, we, yearning in dismay
That their accomplished courses circle out,
Seek also for the journey as each one,
With an unspoken intent, sets abroad.
They also in their distant memories,
Or some immediate impulse governing,
Send back reflections for us : we between
Their sweet desires and our ascendencies
Transfer in gradual change ourselves—and go.

ACQUISITION.

RAPID in action—of enlightened force—
　　A palpitating summons of delight—
Virtuous with energy and feeling will—
Most wonderfully real and exact
Is apprehension—acquisition—the
Attainment of informal spectacles.
Gently distended from inception of
This knowledge, with irradiation soft,
Goes the adjustment of all blending things.
Form may not conquer Spirit, but is made
Daily unequal as the strife goes on :
Still Doubt feeds Time in silence—public—stern—
And Increase goes unmeasured and unknown.

CONTACT.

TH' accumulated stores of deed decay :
  Actions and forms, select accomplices
Of an Occult Design, grow indistinct.
To see material things and thence to draw
Expression, is a passionate delight,
For Beauty strikes into the Soul like fire :
But we are nearer, and diviner come
With an immediate instinct on Design.
Such is creation in us ; whence we give
Bounty more subtle to the things we see
Than in them grows—repeat them and say more.
Down to the heart goes Love and draws thereout
An unshaped Fancy of perpetual joy :
Not time, nor limitation, nor real
Apparentness of any daily thing
Expresses it ; but all the indistinct
Glorious and fruitful haze of hope and belief
Whirl in a combination most redeemed
From mortal fear and interruption of
Possible failure or disastrous end.
There is no form to light—itself becomes
What it is hampered by : so Love expands
In all the beauty of an endless thing—
Outstretching from the heart unformed—unnamed :
Impossible of loss, for contact is
Consolidation, and opposing Shape
Has vanished—for no needless thing remains.

ASSEMBLAGE.

THERE is a unity in Love : because
  Such was the advent when the Soul was set
Outward in apparentness as such,
Knowing that this was its identity.
Soul 's indivisible, but Shape becomes
Simply in service to perpetual chance :
Which terrible issue was when Evil took
Its passionate advantage to destroy
Sweet, gentle Love's unknown accompaniment.
Long revolutions of harsh servitude
That captive went, and is returning back.
Into a thousand desperate Forms compelled
Love forgets all—returning single-eyed.
Back thro' corporeal vicissitudes
Of agony and fury—shape and crime—
Assembling come our Souls ; and Love ahead,
In glorious leadership, exulting sings
The possibility of an exact
And perfect rendering into herself.
All the old formal things of Crime depart ;
Desire, and dark pollution, and sorrows
Of Shape sink down—fall from th' unmixed Soul.
Led by the lost Instructress of the Heart
Reality advances and becomes
A thing of influence and subtle state,
Not any more demanding time and sight.

REALIZATION.

IN all the outspread plains of afterwards
  Love is a gainer, and his day of Time,
However sweet, fades in a flying dawn.
For Man is Space and Woman Light ; and they,
In adaptation of simplicity,
Newly revealed do possibly combine.
Which formless glory sheds upon to-day's
Eager advance beatitude and flight.
Sweet Influence, securely intrenched
With power to work her deeds, looks out and sees
Nearly th' approaching end : calling aloud
All sidelong avenues she presses on—
In gazing over sees not things beside.

EXPRESSION.

WE sometimes see : we feel and blindly hid
　　Lie in ourselves the evidence and proof.
Tho' sullen in their utterance, yet to us
Such are sufficient ; but there comes demand
For guarantee, and we attempt display.
Transmission, interchange, and mighty things
In rude translation issue out, but still
It is impossible to speak as see—
And as we speak the vision disappears.
Sounds of the tongue disturb, and vacant ears
Are not the same as open, credulous eyes.
Yet into speech pure beauty is distilled
And we in silence turn—acquiring more.

FUTURITY.

WOMAN came after man and for a cause :
    He is passivity—recipient—
And citadel to her incoming Soul
Gently in guidance, seeking to enhance
Its adequate brightness into Shape and Form.
His is the Form—seeing herself a Soul
Is safety to her essence, and delight
Of feature is forgotten as he looks,
Startled, upon her Spirit entering in.
The Light is its own guide whither to go :
Shape cannot seize it—but it lightens Shape :
And she is as a flame—burning apart
Only in air—unless she enters in :
Set in her mastery, and being there
Inherited entering another Shape.
Woman is Light—seeing herself as she
Appears in Man—without him all the void
Of unshapen darkness swallows up herself.
Entered there 's never dissolution, nor
Dismemberment, nor ever breakage more,
Nor any other than a single thing
Surviving from the summit's stop of Time
That goes into another reckoning.

SPEECH.

HE sees—his brother not : for this descends
    Into his hands the fearful weight of Speech.
Crushed by the burden thro' some harrowing days
Goes heavily his Soul—cloaking the weight.
Implacable the Powers pile on their gifts
Of knowledge—vision—prophecy and use.
Bent and disfigured thro' the jeering crowd
Treads the o'erladen, incapable of ease.
Despair bursts from his tongue, with arms outspread
More to the Powers than unto men he calls
Such words as the long burden made him know.
How is the issue—how th' affrighted cry ?
Cold Failure with her leaden eyes, and hands
Moist with the breath of those she chills, attends.
Into her face needs go a passionate cry—
Before her visage needs a kindling fire—
Drowning her monotone tremendous tongues
Must ring in daring and in agony.
To these she yields—muffling her sunken head
The mantle of defeat she draws and goes.

Of burden light, gently, O wearied tongue
Speak to the waters of a sinking sea :

Lightly the winds, chained to accustomed ways,
Bear out the Singer's sombre, evening words.
Within himself, passing in bright review,
Go the battalions of a wondrous fray—
Beauty and power—joy, grandeur, and delight
Reward his eyes, and with his words at will
Abroad the world he sends their journeying songs.
Not all—still rooted in unyielding, dumb
Impossible speech lie things of care and grief.

RELEASE.

I SAW by daily suns a giant Bird
   Stand on a minaret by the vacant sea.
On every eastern sky his brooding form,
Defined in darkness, rose against the light.
Day grew in heat, and, turning with the sun,
Th' unlidded eyes gathered unconscious fire.
Eve fell :—red in the sun's retreat, unclosed,
His glaring orbs gazed o'er the weltering seas.
I marvelled :—what mighty chains hung on his
     wings—
High o'er the wondering world what power unknown
Detained his flight ? In fierce, uncovered day
He stood, and lonely in the night, excelled
With patience all the heavenly lamps and stars.
Time passed—he stood. I marvelled not—forgot
His going possible—myself grew old.
I, too, gazed on the going sun and dreamed
Of entering some evening sweet with him
The ready gates that stood so welcome —wide.
So looking from the air commotion fell—
Unusual a shade o'erspread, and as
The sun touched on the Ocean's rim, this Bird
Displayed his mighty sails and journey took—
Left vacant more the seas and minaret.

THE VOICE.

THERE is a dreadful distance can be dreamed
   Remote in awe—glorious in court and spire,
With messengers of beauty, and details
Of harmony to this far world unknown.
Served by the countless syndicate of light
There is a Ruler—housed with power immense,
Whose speech is Influence—whose works are Laws.
Sped from the fashion of His forming hands
Rolled down th' abysmal plain a glittering sphere—
And planets swinging.   Pulsating in the globe
For ages rests an answering desire
Returning to the fashion of His hands.
Over the dreadful distance flies a-wing
Creation with her creatures—circling swift,
All on the darting planets throb betimes
To the long tension of an ancient day
The mighty Word blew far this starry cloud.
Whirled in an undismayed return we go
In light and darkness nearer, while a-stir
Runs the revival thro' a World's desire.
Spirit and Space, Material and Soul
Quiver with waiting—but silent still afar
Is hushed the dreadful welcome of The Voice.
Between the long remoteness of designs
We stand unknowing, but our ears incline
Perchance, affrighted to the Voice that comes.